Raising the Standards of Dating

Raising the Standards of Dating

A Practical Guide to God's View on
Life, Sex, and Self-Worth

CARYLE DECRUISE

Raising the Standards of Dating: A Practical Guide to God's View on Life, Sex, and Self-Worth

Copyright © 2022 by Caryle DeCruise

Published by Cassy's Touch Publishing, LLC
cassystouch.com

Request for information should be addressed to:

Cassy's Touch Publishing, cassystouch.com

Library of Congress Control Number: 2022911032

ISBN: 978-1-7359222-8-7 (paperback)

ISBN: 978-1-7359222-9-4 (ebook)

All Scripture quotations, unless other indicated, are taken from the Holy Bible New International Version®, NIV®. Copyright © 1973, 1978, 1984, 2011 by Biblica, Inc.™ Used by permission.

Scripture quotations taken from the Amplified® Bible (AMPC), Copyright © 1954, 1958, 1962, 1964, 1965, 1987 by The Lockman Foundation. Used by permission. www.lockman.org

All contents of the Common English Bible Web Site are: Copyright 2012 by Common English Bible and/or its suppliers. All rights reserved.

Scripture quotations marked (CEV) are from the Contemporary English Version Copyright © 1991, 1992, 1995 by American Bible Society. Used by Permission.

Scripture quotations marked KJV are taken from the King James Version of the Bible, public domain.

Scripture taken from the New King James Version®. Copyright © 1982 by Thomas Nelson. Used by permission. All rights reserved.

Scripture quotations marked (NLT) are taken from the *Holy Bible*, New Living Translation, copyright ©1996, 2004, 2015 by Tyndale

House Foundation. Used by permission of Tyndale House Publishers, Carol Stream, Illinois 60188. All rights reserved.

Names of persons mentioned within the book are fictitious and do not represent any known person with that name.

Any internet addresses and telephone numbers in this book are offered as a resource. They are not intended in any way to be or imply an endorsement by Cassy's Touch Publishing, nor does Cassy's Touch Publishing vouch for the content of these sites and numbers for the life of this book. Cassy's Touch Publishing is not responsible for websites (or their content) that are not owned by Cassy's Touch Publishing.

No part of this publication may be reproduced, stored in a retrieval system, or transmitted in any form or by any means—electronic, mechanical, photocopy, recording, or any other—without the prior permission of the publisher.

Cover Design: Cassy's Touch Publishing, LLC

Cover Photo: Maya G and Khory Fulton

You can connect with Caryle through her website: genesisqueen.com

Printed in the United States of America

Dedication

I would like to dedicate this book to my Heavenly Father who loves me unconditionally and who would not allow my mistakes to dictate my future. You are wonderful and worthy of all praise. I am forever grateful for who You are and for all You have done. I love You Lord.

Contents

Acknowledgments .... *v*

Introduction: Life Experiences Is Our Greatest Teacher *1*

1 The Impairment of Sex and My Decision to Date God *5*

2 Flesh-Led vs. Spirit-Led *17*

3 Rubies Conduct Themselves As Rubies *29*

4 Is He Equipped to Lead You, and Is She Suitable for You? *37*

5 Beware of These Forevers *49*

6 There's Truth in All of It *63*

7 Speak It, until You Believe It *75*

8 My Truth and More *81*

Prayer *117*

Acknowledgments

To my mother, Sherial, I admire your strength and courage. Thank you for being my superwoman and for your guidance and leadership.

To my dad, Caryle, thank you for your support and listening ear when needed.

To the number one queen in my life, my baby girl, Kendall. Thank you for being great and amazing. It is an honor and blessing to be your mommy and to witness you become everything God has created you to be.

To my siblings, thank you for your love, support, and encouragement during this process. A special thanks to my sister Tamika; thank you for your time and for allowing me to read various chapters to you regardless of the time of day.

To my brother-in-law Corey, thank you for your perspective and encouragement.

To my aunt Tammy, thank you for the race we ran together and the various mic drop moments we shared. We will run together again in the near future.

To my Pastor, Cassandra, you are a true woman of God. Thank you for being available whenever your sheep (especially me) are in need. I appreciate your invaluable feedback and words of encouragement.

To my friend, Mrs. A.M., thank you for being supportive and for completing your homework assignments (inside joke). I truly appreciate your time and dedication.

To my brother in Christ, Dr. Al-Aakhir A. Rogers (teammate), thank you for being the Bible I needed in college and for showing me what a surrendered life to Christ should resemble.

Lastly, to my sisters in Christ, Sommer, and Jocqueline. Sommer, thank you for your kindness and for creating a judgment-free friendship zone. Jocqueline, you made this book possible. Thank you for planting the seed in my spirit through our many conversations regarding sex and dating and how I "should write a book." Well friend, I listened!

Is not wisdom found among the aged? Does not long life bring understanding?

-Job 12:12

Introduction

Life Experiences Is Our Greatest Teacher

Do you know that God has a plan for our lives, and He loves us more than we could fathom? The act of Him sending His Son to die for us (John 3:16) is evidence of how much He truly loves us. Surrendering my life to Christ sooner would have spared me from many unwise decisions I have made over time. Knowing Christ may not prevent someone from ever making a bad decision. However, developing a personal relationship with Christ enables one to make wiser decisions throughout their life.

This book was written as a result of conversations I discussed with my friend pertaining to sex and dating. Although dating is not a biblical term,

I believe it is important to many Christians. The world has overwhelmed us with dating apps, dating books, and even dating shows. Pardon me for adding to the list. I am not a self-proclaimed relationship expert, nor am I a certified counselor; I am simply a young woman sharing my personal experiences and beliefs concerning these matters. As one of my previous pastors stated, "This is my opinion; you can take it or trash it."

Dating can be fun and exciting, yet at the same time, it can also contribute to draining and stressful experiences. Emphasis should be placed on taking heed to godly wisdom versus societal norms when deciding to engage in a dating relationship. Christianity is not void of fun nor confinement to church, work, or home. As Christians, we should strive to be a reflection of God's glory in our dating relationships and our lives in general. Choosing God does not prohibit you from dating, but applying godly wisdom translates into being selective with whom and how you choose to date. I could have avoided many pitfalls along the way had I known then what I know now (sound familiar?), especially as it pertains to dating relationships.

Though the book is geared towards women, men are not excluded and can benefit from this information as well. As you read this book, I pray you will receive a better understanding of who God is and allow Him to become a part of every intricate detail of your life. He's not a God who wants to zap all of the fun and excitement out of your life. He wants you to live abundantly (John 10:10). Granting God unlimited access to your mind and heart will be the best decision you will ever make.

You say, "Food was made for the stomach, and the stomach for food." (This is true, though someday God will do away with both of them.) But you can't say that our bodies were made for sexual immorality. They were made for the Lord, and the Lord cares about our bodies.

-1 Corinthians 6:13 (NLT)

1

The Impairment of Sex and My Decision to Date God

In school, we are informed of the dangers associated with drinking alcohol and the role it plays in impairing our judgment. We are also informed of the risks associated with engaging in unprotected sex, which could result in an unplanned pregnancy or contracting an STD. Although we received the knowledge of the physical aftereffects of engaging in sexual intercourse, there is also a mental aftereffect associated with this act that was unbeknownst to me.

It was not until I became an adult that I realized sex impaired my judgment just like alcohol. This book does not seek to equate that drinking alcohol and sex are the same. The argument is that the aftereffects a person experiences when engaging in either activity are remarkably similar.

Reflect on a prior or current relationship in your life when sex was a factor and how thoughts of reasoning were ignored after your sexual encounter. God designed sex for marriage only between a man and a woman and forbids His children from partaking in carnal relationships. During this time, we often develop an emotional attachment to individuals we probably should have never allowed in our lives from the beginning. Furthermore, we are commanded by God not to engage in sexual immorality (1 Corinthians 6:18), as nothing good will arise from it.

THE SCIENCE OF SEX

In my opinion, during sex, the brain will become helpless to the sexual arousal and gratification the body feels; hence, the individual has become sexually impaired. By reason of sexual impairment, one will become vulnerable to the "blinder and sexual withdrawal" phases described in this chapter. In this altered state of mind, the brain begins to wear external glasses, known as "blinders." When wearing blinders, an individual is oblivious to their thoughts, decisions, and behaviors. I know you are probably saying, "What in the world is she referring to?" Let me explain.

When an individual enters the blinder phase, their insight to decipher what is beneficial or harmful to themselves will greatly diminish. For example, in this phase, a woman may experience difficulty in realizing the man she is sexually involved with has a temper or is a master manipulator. Likewise, a man in the blinder phase may experience difficulty in realizing the woman he is sexually involved with is more concerned with his financial status than him.

Regardless if a person is considered a "good man" or a "good woman," we are not permitted to engage in premarital sex according to the Word of God.

The amount of time an individual chooses to remain in this altered state of mind varies from person to person, as each will most likely experience a "blackout." The blackout period, defined by me, is when an individual is unable to receive rational or sound advice regarding their relationship. Some people have referred to this as "love is blind," and truthfully, red flags are often overlooked when sex is involved.

When blinded, the blinder phase and blackout period are inevitable and influence a person's ability to make rational decisions or receive sound advice. The Bible states in 1 Corinthians 10:13 that God will provide a way out of temptation, meaning He will always prepare an exit door before we engage in any sinful activity. However, we often travel through the door of our choosing, which leads to more trouble. Instead, we should travel through the door God has destined for us.

Shifting gears, let's return to the earlier topic of sexual impairment as it relates to alcohol. If you were ever in the presence of someone who has consumed too much alcohol, you may have noticed a decline in their rational behavior as their alcohol consumption increased. Once the effects of alcohol subside, this individual is capable of making rational decisions again and is no longer considered impaired. Similarly, I believe the same applies to sex. After an individual engages in it (sex), their judgment will become impaired as the frequency of their sexual activity increases. Once the individual refrains from premarital sex, being impaired sexually is no longer a factor, and they too are able to make rational decisions again.

Before becoming impairment-free regarding sex, I believe an individual will enter into the sexual withdrawal phase (yes, there's another phase) and experience a revelation. During the revelation, the individual will state, "Man, this situation I am in is so unhealthy for me" (and here's the but), "but I can't seem to leave them alone." The reason behind this is simple; the individual is experiencing sexual withdrawals. To obtain their fix or stop their cravings, they will return to the person they are sexually involved with. Thus, proving the flesh is only satisfied temporarily until the next craving occurs.

Lastly, once detached from your sexual partner(s), you may have asked yourself the following questions or even stated the following comments, "Man, what was I thinking? Or, how did I not see them for the snake they truly were? Or, I should have never given them my number in the first place. Or, I should have never wasted my time with them." These are examples of sober-minded afterthoughts we have most likely experienced throughout our dating history.

DATING WITH GOD (DWG)

In my desire to deny history the ability to repeat itself in my life by experiencing hurt, pain, and sober-minded afterthoughts, I informed my friend that we should start "Dating Our Daddy," meaning God. Eventually, I changed the concept to "Dating With God" (DWG). This concept is simple, rewarding, and sacrificial at the same time. DWG is precisely that—a decision to date the Heavenly Father for an extended period of time, as you allow Him to heal you and cleanse you from any prior hurt or pain in your life. To date God, you must start by removing relationships that interfere with or hinder your goals in life and overall well-being. Additionally, avoid becoming involved with anyone new during this process, as you should remain single and available to God.

During your alone time with God, He will begin to download pertinent information to you concerning your life. The Bible states, "Before I formed you in the womb I knew you" (Jeremiah 1:5). Your alone time with the Father will greatly benefit you as you begin to trust Him with your life. You never lose when you choose Jesus; you lose when you do not.

The concept of dating God is impactful and life-altering and should not be considered a punishment for the inability to "get" a man or a woman. To appreciate the journey you are on, you must shift your mind to a better place and begin to enjoy the decluttering process of your inner being. Do not allow opposing family members or friends to discourage you from embarking on this journey. Your decision to choose purity over satisfying your fleshly desires is admirable and pleasing unto the Lord.

The DWG journey is different for everyone, and the timeframe will vary. From a practical standpoint, dating God could mean a commitment of six months, a year, or even longer. As for me, I followed the DWG concept for an entire year after my marriage ended. Once my year was complete, I decided to continue dating God until He said otherwise. Regardless of the selected timeframe, make certain to welcome the new you.

During my journey, I decided to write this book and began to experience a peace that is found in God alone (2 Thessalonians 3:16). My experience was remarkable and spiritually enlightening, and I encourage you to embrace continual growth in Christ as well. True joy and contentment were birthed once I became isolated, which created a level of elevation while preventing a degree of stagnation at the same time. I did not become a recluse, but my mindset and actions had to change in order to experience something different and transformational.

Of course, I was tempted and desired to date a fine man during my year of dating God, but I would have been cheating on Him. When you are in a committed relationship with someone, neither party is allowed to date another individual; or at least you shouldn't (just saying). Therefore, I had to develop that same concept with God. Allowing a third party to enter into your committed relationship with the Father is equivalent to cheating on Him. This is not a "poor me" situation. It is a decision to remove all distractions to focus on the Lord. You are entitled to spend your time with whomever you desire, but make certain to spend time with the ultimate giver of life, Jesus Christ.

So put to death *and* deprive of power the evil longings of your earthly body [with its sensual, self-centered instincts] immorality, impurity, *sinful* passion, evil desire, and greed, which is [a kind of] idolatry [because it replaces your devotion to God].

-Colossians 3:5 (AMP)

2

Flesh-Led vs. Spirit-Led

I would like to expound upon a shared belief adopted from society where we perceive our knowledge and understanding of a person is enhanced after maintaining an intimate (premarital sex) relationship with them. In doing so lies the difficulty in determining if a man or woman enjoys the individual or the pleasurable encounters (sex) associated with the person. Sexual intercourse should not be the determinative factor guiding the decision for a person to remain or depart from one's life. It is essential for a person to apply wiser methods to determine their interest in someone, aside from engaging in what is considered society's sexual norm.

THE CAUSE AND EFFECT OF BECOMING ONE

Past generations (grandparents) embraced the beauty of knowing someone spiritually and intellectually, yet our current generation believes this form of intimacy is old-fashioned and outdated. Whenever I allowed myself to be led by the flesh and not by the Spirit of God, the outcome often left me hurt and disappointed. The Bible states, "Flesh gives birth to flesh, but the Spirit gives birth to spirit" (John 3:6). A different version states, "Humans give life to their children. Yet only God's Spirit can change you into a child of God" (CEV). These Scripture references, like many others, have provided the blueprint to winning in life and what is required to live by the Spirit of God and not by the flesh. In fact, our moments of sexual climax (led by the flesh) we share with someone outside of marriage fail to reveal the aftermath of our consequences.

When engaging in sex, "Don't you know that your bodies are parts of Christ? So then, should I take parts of Christ and make them a part of someone who is sleeping around? No way! Don't you know that anyone who is joined to someone who is sleeping around is one body with that person? The scripture says, *The two will become one flesh*" (1 Corinthians 6:15-16 CEB). Many people have defined such connections as soul ties. In essence, we become one with each individual we choose to sleep with. Consequently, we unknowingly create or created "marriage-like" relationships by joining ourselves to those currently or to those from our past. Sex was created by God for a husband and wife and allows them to "become one flesh" (Genesis 2:24). To break the connections we have formed through premarital sex, we must repent and pray for our healing. As a result, we can establish and maintain healthy dating relationships in the future.

WHO IS YOUR ARCHITECT?

Now that we understand how we become one with others, I would like to focus on the importance of allowing Christ to be the foundation of our dating relationships. When Christ is our foundation, we can prevent the above connections (marriage-like relationships) from occurring. Therefore, let's examine the difference in our home-building process compared to the home-building process of God Almighty. We as women are influenced by the customs of this world and may believe homes are primarily built through relationships involving sex. Men are also influenced by said customs and may believe part of their identity will be found in the bedroom.

Unfortunately, we begin to build our homes with material I call "lustful quicksand," indicative of our sinking relationship status the moment we partake in sex as a single person. A sinking relationship is also equivalent to a building that was constructed without the proper foundation...at some point, it will collapse. More importantly, the Bible states, "Without the help of the LORD it is useless to build a home or to guard a city" (Psalm 127:1 CEV). Use the Word of God as the foundation for your life and avoid establishing a home that does not include Him.

Most dating relationships perceive intimacy as being accomplished through sex only. It is normal for an individual to desire intimacy with their significant other. Nevertheless, why does the removal of clothing seem to solidify the relationship? For this reason, we fail to recognize society's method of dating invites a monster into our lives, sin masquerading in the form of intimacy. Sex wreaks havoc in the lives of those who partake in it outside of its original purpose for mankind (husband and wife). Jesus, however, spoke of a different level of intimacy when He stated, "Abide in Me, and I in you. As the branch cannot bear fruit of itself, unless it abides in the vine, neither can you, unless you abide in Me" (John 15:4 NKJV). The intimacy Christ spoke of explains how we must abide in Him in Word and deed to experience an incomparable degree of intimacy.

For God to become the architect in our dating relationships, we must read, understand and apply His Word to our lives daily to remain sexually pure. Above all, "Don't you realize that your body is the temple of the Holy Spirit, who lives in you and was given to you by God? You do not belong to yourself" (1 Corinthians 6:19 NLT). The Bible also reveals the price that was paid for us by stating, "You were bought with a price [you were actually purchased with the precious blood of Jesus and made His own]. So then, honor *and* glorify God with your body"(1 Corinthians 6:20 AMP).

Not only were we "purchased with the precious blood of Jesus," but we were also created for God's glory, according to Isaiah 43:7, which means our lives should reflect His glory. We do not have the liberty to do as we choose with our bodies (contrary to popular belief), specifically when it involves participating in sin. We must surrender our lives to Jesus Christ and live as we are commanded to. Furthermore, "If you try to hang on to your life, you will lose it. But if you give up your life for my sake, you will save it" (Matthew 16:25 NLT).

SLEEPING WITH THE ENEMY

When living according to our flesh, it also becomes our number one enemy relative to premarital sex or any sin in that regard. Thus, proving the importance of being led by the Spirit versus the flesh.

We are commanded to "Flee from sexual immorality. All other sins a person commits are outside the body, but whoever sins sexually, sins against their own body" (1 Corinthians 6:18). In addition to becoming impaired by sex, one will remain captive to it through continual acts of sinning against their own body. Though a person cannot "get rid of" themselves, so to speak, they can avert future soul ties with sexual partners they are not married to.

The Bible also states, "but each person is tempted when they are dragged away by their own evil desire and enticed. Then, after desire has conceived, it gives birth to sin; and sin, when it is full-grown, gives birth to death" (James 1:14–15). This Scripture provides a clear timeline of what transpires from start to finish within a person's life concerning sin. The starting point results from one's internal desire, the flesh (our number one enemy), and ends in one's death. I interpret such death as a few things, the most obvious being a physical death. Another death could insinuate a spiritual death and forfeiting the blessings God has in store for them by continuing to live in sin.

Although God is forgiving, He is also very serious about His Word and does not want His children to experience sex without the commitment of marriage. I get it; most people do not desire to be married, which is perfectly fine. However, there is no ambiguity in the Word of God as it pertains to His command not to engage in sexual immorality. Since God is the creator of sex, we must all abide by His rulebook, the Bible.

God's grace and mercy provide us with an opportunity to align our lives to His will. I am neither judging nor condemning anyone, but it is time for us to live for our Creator, who loves us unconditionally.

Satan is bold and brazen, showcasing his daily sinful agendas as the norm. Children of God, we must take a stance and represent God's Kingdom and proclaim His agendas of holiness and sexual purity. Besides, "The world is passing away, and with it its lusts [the shameful pursuits and ungodly longings]; but the one who does the will of God *and* carries out His purposes lives forever" (1 John 2:17 AMP).

You are the one who put me together inside my mother's body, and I praise you because of the wonderful way you created me. Everything you do is marvelous! Of this I have no doubt. Nothing about me is hidden from you! I was secretly woven together out of human sight, but with your own eyes you saw my body being formed. Even before I was born, you had written in your book everything about me.

-Psalm 139:13-16 (CEV)

3

Rubies Conduct Themselves As Rubies

Queens, when God created you, He was intentional, diligent, and delicate throughout the entire process. Proverbs 31:10 asks, "Who can find a virtuous woman? for her price *is* far above rubies" (KJV). The value bestowed upon you from the beginning of time will always remain the same "above rubies." Therefore, attempts made by others to diminish your worth as a woman will prove to be futile by cause of God's perfect plan.

Since God created us (women), we should conduct ourselves with standards that reflect our worth as a ruby. Our speech and the behavior we display should validate His hard work amid the process of creating a woman. For those unfamiliar with rubies, they are one of the most expensive stones and are rarer than most diamonds. The rare jewel whom God speaks of will not engage in unbecoming behavior, portraying herself as ungodly and unladylike. The Scripture does not state she is impossible to find, but it asks, "Who can find a virtuous woman?" This woman does exist, but she is very rare.

Coupled with being priced above a rare jewel, the virtuous woman of Proverbs 31 verses 10–31 lacks nothing in value and wears dignity and strength as her garments. She brings good to her husband and not harm. She speaks with wisdom and refuses to engage in idleness. She is kind and gentle and works diligently to ensure those attached to her are cared for, in addition to those she encounters. She is a beautiful woman who understands her outward appearance is no match for her inner beauty. She receives praise and accolades from her family, and most importantly, she fears the Lord and her work will bring her praise at the city gates.

THE TWO ARE NOT THE SAME

Understanding the value bestowed upon you will strengthen and empower you, but the lack of understanding concerning your worth will mirror your decision-making ability and personal relationships. From a dating standpoint, when your worth is unknown, you may believe that your validation as a woman will occur once you become involved in a relationship with a man. You may also settle for less than ideal relationships when your worth is unknown. A man may also believe that his involvement in a relationship with you has somehow added value to you as a woman.

I am not suggesting a good man would not be helpful to you in many ways; what I am implying is for you to acknowledge the first Man who bestowed value upon your life. The woman God created is beautiful, strong, and "worth far above rubies." Furthermore, the idea that your worth is based primarily on a relationship status is absurd and directly conflicts with God's original design.

LEAD BY EXAMPLE

Knowing your worth is a head and heart matter and involves teaching others how to respect you while conducting themselves around you. Address inappropriate actions/comments from others immediately. Setting the standard for your treatment is required to establish and maintain the level of respect you are worth. Your actions and standards will reveal the love that exudes from within.

Rubies Conduct Themselves As Rubies

Indeed, self-love is the greatest when you love yourself first and will ensure your mental/emotional stability as people depart from your life or vice versa. Loving yourself more than a significant other speaks volumes to your level of self-admiration and self-respect. Likewise, I once informed an ex that he underestimated the love I have for myself versus the love I gave to him. It is dangerous to allow a relationship, titles, degrees, or material items to define you. Once those items or people disappear, you inevitably become trapped in the past. After being trapped, you believe the essence of who you are is lost, failing to realize that you are a rare jewel created by God.

Leading by example in action can also be accomplished through speech. Instead of waiting to hear a man express how beautiful and intelligent she is, a woman can lead the charge and state these things to herself. The desire a woman has to listen to a man whisper "sweet nothings" is perfectly fine and normal. However, a man's words should never be used as a substitute for how God can make a woman feel. The Word of God informs us that we are beautiful, strong, wise, and loved. If God has stated these truths, why walk in disbelief concerning them?

When we as women have an unhealthy sense of our self-worth, we unconsciously pass these harmful perceptions from generation to generation. Subsequently, we create little angels who seek validation and worth in things or people instead of God. Developing a personal relationship with the Lord will help you discover and love yourself on a level no man can exceed. Again, I am not implying a good man would not be of benefit to you; I am stressing the importance of knowing your self-worth before a good man arrives. It's simple, your worth and the essence of who you are as a woman is intertwined with God Almighty.

Run from anything that stimulates youthful lusts. Instead, pursue righteous living, faithfulness, love, and peace. Enjoy the companionship of those who call on the Lord with pure hearts.

-2 Timothy 2:22 (NLT)

4

Is He Equipped to Lead You, and Is She Suitable for You?

Men and women alike are known for constructing a list of non-negotiables and qualifying factors before meeting "the one." Drafting a list of must-haves is excellent; nevertheless, the list should not focus on superficial qualities which lack real substance. The first part of this chapter will outline what the list entails for women, followed by what it entails for men. In life, we tend to allow superficial versus substantial attributes of a person to determine their presence in our lives, and the difference should be distinguished.

Raising the Standards of Dating

Ladies, do not become overly concerned with a man's physical build and bank account. Often overlooked is his driver's license, and by that, I mean his spiritual driver's license. Let me explain this analogy. A man possesses two different driver's licenses: one obtained from the Department of Motor Vehicles and one from heaven, acquired from God. Both licenses require driving capabilities in the natural and in the spiritual.

The natural license requires proficient knowledge of the driving rules and the ability to comprehend road signs. A spiritual driver's license requires a man to spend quality time with God as he develops and matures in his relationship with the Father. The ability to acquire a spiritual license and where a man (the one) will lead/drive you (woman) in life as it pertains to the Word of God should be of more concern than his physical build and money. The desire for such wants is understandable; however, they should not take precedence over the spiritual qualities of a man.

TRAITS OF A SPIRITUAL LICENSE

Consider the following qualities to determine if he is equipped to lead you:

- his ability to provide and protect you
- his ability to make sacrifices for you
- his ability to respect and honor you
- his ability to be gentle with you
- his ability to be patient and kind with you
- his ability to have and display self-control
- his understanding of the vision for his life
- his willingness to submit to godly leadership

It is often said the two most important decisions you will ever make in life are accepting Jesus Christ as your Lord and Savior and deciding who to marry (if you desire to do so). "The head of the woman is man"

(1 Corinthians 11:3), and for that reason, ladies, be mindful of the leadership you decide to place yourself under. Review his spiritual driver's license carefully to determine if he's equipped to be the driver/leader in your life. Be observant of how he speaks to you and treats you in public, behind closed doors, and how he honors you regarding your body. If your decision to remain sexually pure is not embraced and respected in your dating relationship, then remove yourself and continue in your pursuit of holiness.

Additionally, date a man who is capable of sharing the Word of God with you as he leads you closer to Christ. The Bible asks, "Can two people walk together without agreeing on the direction?" (Amos 3:3 NLT). The Bible also states, "Do not be unequally bound together with unbelievers [do not make mismatched alliances with them, inconsistent with your faith]. For what partnership can righteousness have with lawlessness? Or what fellowship can light have with darkness?" (2 Corinthians 6:14 AMP). These Scriptures signify the importance of making wise decisions regarding who we allow in our lives. They are especially important regarding the man you believe is equipped to lead you.

On the other hand, men have often complained about a woman's inability to follow their lead. A woman was created to help, and under optimal conditions, women are capable of following their lead (man). However, hesitancy may set in when the visionary (man) is unclear of his plans and direction in life for family and a future. That said, do not become the person the Bible describes in James 1:8 as *"being* a double-minded man, unstable *and* restless in all his ways [in everything he thinks, feels, or decides]" (AMP). Decisions are made best when plans are established. Hence, do not "pass the time" with a woman, but define your plan of action to assure her of your ability to lead and provide for her.

IS SHE SUITABLE FOR YOU?

Men, when deciding which woman to wed, a review of her qualities is also imperative. Women are not considered the driver of their relationship and were given the title of helper by God. For this reason, a woman should possess helper qualities. I encourage you to exercise patience and seek God's help during this process, while women are advised to echo the same sentiment.

Determining a woman's advancement to the next chapter (marriage) in a man's life is often wagered on "sexual test-drives." This concept is society-driven and was never God's plan for His children. Though we have normalized lustful trials and errors (sin), this behavior is inappropriate when we place trust and confidence in God. He is the creator of sex and understands the significance of us partaking in this act once married.

Ultimately, He supplies and provides for our needs and wants. Focusing primarily on a woman's beauty and body rather than her inner attributes is the result of being led by the flesh versus the Spirit of God. The Bible states, "Charm is deceptive, and beauty does not last; but a woman who fears the LORD will be greatly praised" (Proverbs 31:30 NLT). True beauty lies within the heart and spirit of a person.

Consider the following qualities to determine if she is suitable for you:

- her ability to be a helper
- her willingness to be led by you
- her ability to respect you as a man
- her ability to be kind and patient
- her ability to have and display self-control
- her willingness to submit to godly leadership

- how nurturing she is
- how diligent she is
- how encouraging she is
- how compassionate she is

These are excellent qualities for a potential wife to possess, as some may believe the greatest amongst these is her willingness to be led and her ability to respect you as a man. The lack of said qualities will alter the dynamics of any relationship and give rise to women taking the lead. A woman who decides to lead will ultimately create an environment of chaos and confusion, thereby shifting the roles within the relationship. Before becoming upset with the messenger, let me explain. If marriage is your desire, having a godly understanding of your responsibilities before your wedding day is important. Husband and wife roles through the lens of society are vastly different from God's design of a husband and wife.

Is He Equipped to Lead You, and Is She Suitable for You?

God's intention for the man and woman regarding purpose and roles within marriage states, "So the LORD God took the man [He had made] and settled him in the Garden of Eden to cultivate and keep it" (Genesis 2:15 AMP). Adam was the first person to receive instructions from God regarding his purpose in life, signifying the importance of a man understanding God's vision for his own life before pursuing a wife. Three verses down, God said, "It is not good (beneficial) for the man to be alone; I will make him a helper [one who balances him—a counterpart who is] suitable *and* complementary for him" (Genesis 2:18 AMP). The Bible also instructs husbands to love their wives, just as Christ loved the church (Ephesians 5:25).

The role of a wife in regards to being a helper to her husband is often frowned upon and causes many eye-rolling moments when discussed, but it is in our best interest to regard God's Word as true. Being a helper does not mean a wife is less than her husband, but rather his life partner. Indeed, this does not imply that marital problems will not exist because they will; however, applying godly wisdom will benefit those who desire to marry. Concerning wisdom, the Bible states, "Know that [skillful and godly] wisdom is [so very good] for your life *and* soul; If you find wisdom, then there will be a future *and* a reward, And your hope *and* expectation will not be cut off" (Proverbs 24:14 AMP).

Though regarded as a helper, men, ensure you pursue a woman who is suitable and complementary for you as it pertains to your purpose in life. As a man who understands God's divine assignment, be mindful of those who oppose His plan for your life. Once purpose is understood, remove yourself from relationships (especially dating relationships) that will delay you from reaching your destiny; this applies to women as well. The list as it relates to "the one" is a guide to provide assistance, but surely godly wisdom and Scripture references surpass all.

So in everything, do to others what you would have them do to you, for this sums up the Law and the Prophets.

-Matthew 7:12

5

Beware of These Forevers

When we envision spending forever with the one we love, our thoughts are usually on the happier end of the spectrum. However, addressed are the terms "forever girlfriend" and "forever fiancée," which may cause more pain than happiness for some. I define both terms as a woman who realizes her relationship will not yield the expected outcome she hoped for.

As a girlfriend, she has given her all throughout the relationship with her male counterpart, only to realize she will not receive a ring in the end. The fiancée has also remained committed to the relationship and realizes she will not become a wife to her fiancé in the end. To be honest, we often remain in certain relationships longer than we should, and in many instances, we miss our window of opportunity to leave.

TIME SPENT WITH MICHAEL

Described above is what transpired in the life of Nia, a wonderful queen who identified with being a forever girlfriend and a forever fiancée. For privacy reasons, I will only share certain aspects of her story. As a child, Nia was adventurous and creative. She was loved by many and was known for having a kind and gentle spirit. In her twenties, she began a relationship with Michael, whom she dated for several years. Michael and Nia loved each other and often spoke of their long-term goals of purchasing a home and starting a family.

Nia and Michael did everything together, such as travel, have date nights, and alternate between family vacations during Thanksgiving and Christmas. Both families loved one another and wanted the best for the seemingly happy couple. However, after dating for three years, Nia suspected Michael of cheating when he changed the password to his cellular device and refused to provide the new code. He never explained why he changed the code and often started small arguments to avoid discussing the matter. Michael's drastic change created sexual intimacy problems within their relationship, which further cemented Nia's suspicions.

  Despite her intuition, Nia decided to stay with Michael. Though red flags were present, the couple purchased their first home together and were engaged a few years later. Nia was thrilled and believed the engagement was a sign their relationship would develop in the right direction.

As the pair continued to work through their issues, family members and friends were ecstatic and could hardly wait for the wedding day. The engagement lasted four long years, which resulted in Nia becoming a forever fiancée. During that time, she often drew closer to God and desired to please Him instead of others. The decision to draw closer to God was an excellent choice, but there was one major hurdle standing in her way...Michael. Although he believed in God, he was not ready to commit his life to God, which hindered them from growing together in the Lord. Hence her hurdle.

At this juncture, Nia became overwhelmed with the myriad of problems within their relationship and knew the possibility of becoming Michael's wife was diminishing. Much to her surprise, she found the strength to leave, but there was another hurdle...their home. Michael nor Nia was willing to leave the residence and eventually became roommates sleeping in separate quarters of the home. Nia was hurt by their separation and did not want to inform her family and friends, but overall, those closest to her were very supportive.

TIME SPENT WITH WILLIAM

Nia and Michael's unsettling, but not uncommon, living arrangement lasted a year before Nia began dating William. She informed William of her current situation with her ex-Michael from the beginning of their relationship. William also mentioned a female friend he would occasionally speak to and assured Nia the relationship was strictly platonic. After a few months into her new relationship, Nia and Michael reached a financial agreement regarding their home. This agreement allowed Nia to sever all material ties to Michael.

In her new relationship, Nia noticed a stark difference in the treatment she received from Michael compared to her treatment from William. They dated for several years with the hope of one day becoming husband and wife. William was the total opposite of Michael, or at least she thought, which was a major plus. He (William) was goal-oriented, ambitious, and most importantly, he loved the Lord. They attended church gatherings together, read the Bible, and prayed for one another. These were matters of the heart Nia could not share or experience with Michael during their time together.

Marriage discussions began very early in her relationship with William, and both appeared ready to embrace a blissful union. However, a few years into their relationship, his behavior changed. William's subtle changes were apparent to Nia as his attempts to remain discreet became increasingly obvious. The changes consisted of fewer phone calls made to Nia throughout the day and less quality time spent together. William eventually explained to Nia that the changes in his behavior stemmed from work-related issues.

Nia was skeptical, considering work never interfered with their relationship in the past. When confronted, William rejected her claims and assured her that he would not do anything to hurt her. Their relationship lasted for several years, with marriage discussions often ending in an argument, and at this point, Nia was confused. She did not understand how William claimed to love her, but was hesitant to move toward the next chapter in their lives (marriage). Nia eventually dismissed the idea of marrying William and believed they would separate at some point.

Their separation occurred sooner than expected when William confessed to dating Nia and his "platonic friend" simultaneously. Nia was shocked and hurt by the news and realized William's inability to commit to their relationship was no fault of her own. After the revelation, which also created sexual intimacy issues for the couple, William was torn between the two. Nia gave him an ultimatum to decide if a future with her was indeed his desire. In the end, she decided to leave the relationship and looked forward to embracing the new chapter in her life.

Nia was aware that her actions and beliefs regarding dating would require a change in her lifestyle to live according to the Word of God. Although she and William professed their love for Jesus Christ, they fell into their old patterns of sin like many of us. The Bible states that God is married to His "backsliding children" (Jeremiah 3:14 NKJV) when we fall into sin. Though married to us, once we have sinned, we must repent and yield to the promptings of the Holy Spirit to reflect a new life that was changed by Christ (2 Corinthians 5:17 NLT).

OUT WITH THE TWO OLDS, IN WITH THE NEW ONE

After refocusing her priorities in life, a positive turn of events led to Nia becoming a wife to an amazing man. She is grateful to God for blessing her with a husband, who loves, honors, and respects her and the love they share for one another. Regardless of the trials and tribulations she has endured, Nia believes each one served a purpose. Her advice for women is to persevere and fight for people worth fighting for. She also wants women to know that God's love is unconditional and although she is not perfect (none of us are), she strives daily to please Him.

WOMAN TO WOMAN

Nia is truly remarkable, and I appreciate her courage and willingness to share her testimony. Most women reading this chapter can probably relate to Nia's life experiences in more ways than one. Many of us began dating very seriously in our early twenties and eventually fell in love or fell in lust. Like Nia, we also experienced the good, the bad, and the ugly. The desire to become a wife and start a family with the man you love is a common desire amongst most women. However, becoming a wife could be delayed when wife benefits are offered while remaining a girlfriend or fiancée.

When dating, do precisely that, date without including the sexual component. Unfortunately, we have adopted worldly customs and believe dating relationships that do not include sex is cruel and unrealistic. As a single woman (not married), become familiar with the man you are dating and do not perform wifely duties during this time. Performing such duties without the actual title (wife) is equivalent to being a supportive friend who remains loyal through the good times and the bad times.

Indeed, things in life will occur that may not yield a perfect outcome. However, when you are able to control the situation, definitely do so. Take matters slowly and avoid making life decisions with someone when you are sexually impaired.

If you desire to become a wife and have a family of your own one day, then "Beware of These Forevers" and reject societal norms of what a family unit should resemble. God is the creator of families, and we should strive to create homes that embody His original design. The first family that God created is found in Genesis, the first book of the Bible. Quite frankly, we have drifted away from the truth, which is the Word of God, that our swift return to His teachings is imperative for the betterment of our souls. There are great pleasures and benefits in living life according to the Word of God compared to the acceptance of societal norms.

The decision a man and woman make before God as they vow to commit themselves to one another in holy matrimony is sacred and serves as God's plan for sexual relations between a man and a woman. Marriage is known as a sharpening tool and helps couples (man and woman) reflect the image of Christ. Marriage is also the ultimate test of self-denial as we are instructed to consider others above ourselves (Philippians 2:3), including a spouse. Additionally, the Bible states, "He who finds a wife finds what is good and receives favor from the LORD" (Proverbs 18:22). Ladies, you are your husband's "good," especially when you are "good to him every day" of your life (Proverbs 31:12 CEV).

For you have been called to live in freedom, my brothers and sisters. But don't use your freedom to satisfy your sinful nature. Instead, use your freedom to serve one another in love.

-Galatians 5:13 (NLT)

6

There's Truth in All of It

Addressed within this chapter are various topics such as God's timing, a woman's "scientific clock," dating, reasons for settling, self-control, and who is responsible for sexual purity. "For I know the plans I have for you, declares the LORD, plans to prosper you and not to harm you, plans to give you hope and a future" (Jeremiah 29:11). In addition to the Jeremiah verse, Scripture desires for us to prosper in every aspect of our lives by stating, "Beloved, I pray that you may prosper in all things and be in health, just as your soul prospers" (3 John 1:2 NKJV). The ability to prosper in all areas of our lives is a blessing from God and should be considered as such.

GOD'S TIMING

When waiting to receive a gift from God, we must remain mindful of the difference between His timing and our timing. "Nevertheless, do not let this one *fact* escape your notice, beloved, that with the Lord one day is like a thousand years, and a thousand years is like one day" (2 Peter 3:8 AMP). The gifts we receive are an indication of God's timing being perfected in our lives. According to James 1:17, "Whatever is good and perfect is a gift coming down to us from God our Father, who created all the lights in the heavens. He never changes or casts a shifting shadow" (NLT).

These gifts will come forth in the earthly realm in the fullness of time. More notably, "He has made everything beautiful in its time. He has also set eternity in the human heart; yet no one can fathom what God has done from beginning to end" (Ecclesiastes 3:11). Our timing suggests we should attain or accomplish certain things in life by a specific age. However, Scripture states that God "has made everything beautiful in its time." The maturation process of all things in life is essential, and we should not rush to receive something or someone while it or they are still in the infancy stage of development.

MAN-MADE SCIENTIFIC CLOCK

God's gifts have an arrival date and time attached to them, which is known by Him alone. Addressed in this section is your "time clock," as mentioned in the introduction, and will refute society's implication that your age has reduced your possibility of becoming a wife. Unfortunately, the belief in such a myth allows you to accept anyone into your life. Accepting this myth also drives the narrative of feeling you will "grow old alone." Though you may never admit to believing this, your actions and the company you keep reflect the current state of your inner thoughts. All hope should not be lost, as He has promised to give you hope (Jeremiah 29:11).

Ultimately, God knows the desires of our hearts and dictates His plans and timing for our lives. We are instructed to "Take delight in the LORD, and he will give you the desires of your heart" (Psalm 37:4); and while you "Commit your way to the LORD, Trust also in Him, And He shall bring *it* to pass" (Psalm 37:5 NKJV). The Bible also states, "Don't worry about anything; instead, pray about everything. Tell God what you need, and thank him for all he has done" (Philippians 4:6 NLT). Simply put, trust God with your desires and concerns while making your requests known to Him in prayer.

Patiently wait for His perfect choice and allow Him to join you with the man He has selected for you. "Therefore what God has joined together, let no one separate" (Mark 10:9). We (women) are called helper by God and assigned to help the man He has chosen for us. He stated, "It is not good (beneficial) for the man to be alone; I will make him a helper [one who balances him—a counterpart who is] suitable *and* complementary for him" (Genesis 2:18 AMP). Take heart in knowing you are a beautiful helper regardless of your age, but ensure you are helping the right one (man).

DATING SERIOUSLY

When deciding to date seriously with the hope of becoming a beautiful helper, keep these questions in mind, "Can you envision yourself marrying this person? Or is this individual someone you choose to spend time with until 'Mr. Right' arrives?" If you do not foresee marriage with this individual, avoid wasting valuable time you will never redeem, particularly if becoming a wife is your desire. Investing time and energy into the wrong one (person) during a relationship can be exhausting. Be cognizant of the other person's feelings when dating, especially if you do not desire to commit to a long-term relationship; this applies to men as well.

Settling for an individual should not become an option either. Have you ever wondered if your progression in life was delayed or hindered on account of the company you keep as it pertains to relationships? Women may settle for suboptimal relationships, which can attribute to complacency or familiarity with the other person. Loneliness and issues of insecurity are additional motives denoting reasons to remain in said relationships. The ability to recognize and accept ownership of the root cause of a problem is the first step to deliverance from stagnant relationships.

SWEETIE, THIS IS NOT OKAY

The following examples (questions) are life situations of women who may have settled, thereby creating their suboptimal situation. Ladies, who said it was okay to settle for a man who strings you along because he can't decide if he wants to build a future with you or not? Who said it was okay to settle for a man who stays out all night and rarely comes home? Who said it was okay to settle for a man who curses you and the kids on a daily basis? Who said it was okay to settle for a man who puts his hands on you in a violent manner? Who said it was okay to settle for a man who uses your body to feed his sexual appetite? Who said it was okay to settle for a man who constantly cheats on you?

Although rhetorical, examine the above questions closely if they pertain to you. God's daughters are special to Him, and settling for "less than the best" is not an option. Furthermore, violence is never okay, as a man should uplift you and protect you emotionally; if not, leave him and the relationship behind. If you believe the Scripture, "He who finds a wife finds what is good and receives favor from the LORD" (Proverbs 18:22), then believe you are a good woman waiting to be found.

FOOD FOR THOUGHT

Ladies, when the man described in Proverbs 18:22 "finds" you, leave something to the imagination. This idea has become archaic, and as a queen, it is fitting to give our king something to "look forward to." A woman's most sought-after and prized possession is her cookie. Remaining sexually pure when dating is challenging and uncommon, but very beautiful in the eyes of the Lord. The ability to control sexual urges while dating is no easy feat.

We must align our thoughts to the Word of God as we strive to raise our standards by which we live. Sin delivers pleasures we all enjoy, and such pleasures are described in the Bible as fleeting (Hebrews 11:25), meaning the enjoyment of sin is short-lived. The most precious attribute and gift we can present to our significant other while dating is the gift of self-control, which applies to both men and women.

Living in a microwave society has created the desire for instant gratification and the need to control and possess situations to our advantage when deemed necessary. As a result, we often overlook the fundamentals required to attain our desired goals. The lack of godly wisdom during our home-building process further deters us.

For example, marriage may not be a priority when the prize (sought-after gift) has been given away during the dating relationship. When we (women) raise our standards by maintaining sexual purity and refuse to play house (shacking up), men will begin to notice the shift in our lifestyle and respond according to our standards. Remember the adage, "people treat you the way you treat yourself."

HOLINESS IS GENDERLESS

Though women are encouraged to leave something to the imagination, men are **NOT** excluded from maintaining sexual purity, as they too are accountable for their actions. Society has publicly praised and glorified men for their sexual conquests while shaming women for the same behavior. The acceptance of this double standard shall not negate God's command to remain sexually pure. Countless and nameless sexual flings with women are foolish to be perceived or used as the standard to define one as a "manly man" or "stellar guy." Even if the practice (sex) is safe, "It is God's will that you should be sanctified: that you should avoid sexual immorality; that each of you should learn to control your own body in a way that is holy and honorable, not in passionate lust like the pagans, who do not know God" (1 Thessalonians 4:3–5). The Bible is clear regarding holiness, as both men and women are commanded to be holy just as God is holy (1 Peter 1:16).

The LORD is my strength and my [impenetrable] shield; My heart trusts [with unwavering confidence] in Him, and I am helped; Therefore my heart greatly rejoices, And with my song I shall thank Him *and* praise Him.

-Psalm 28:7 (AMP)

7

Speak It, until You Believe It

The pressures of life and the opinions of others can be mentally and emotionally taxing, often consuming our minds and emotions. When we become consumed by such things, we shift our focus from God and allow ourselves to become burdened. Though consumed by the cares of this world, "Give all your worries and cares to God, for he cares about you" (1 Peter 5:7 NLT). Thankfully, the Word of God is our lifeline and point of reference for all things true concerning our lives.

YOU ARE A WINNER

Every morning God blesses you with another day of life; remember you are more than a conqueror

(Romans 8:37), and you can live life in abundance (John 10:10). Without a doubt, both hard times and sad times will hit your doorstep, which could be your current situation. Irrespective of the place or season you are in, use the Word of God to declare victory and blessings over your life.

Think, when Jesus was led by the Spirit to be tempted by Satan in the wilderness, He defeated him (Satan) with the Word of God. The Bible never described a time when Jesus used His fists to fight Satan. Jesus' temptation is revealed in Matthew 4:1–11, and each time He stated to Satan, "It is written" (NKJV), meaning stand firm and fight your enemies by using the Word of God. Satan is not afraid of you per se, but he is afraid of God, and the Word of God, as demons "tremble in terror" (James 2:19 NLT). Be comforted in knowing that all things concerning you is written in the Word of God.

"I AM" AFFIRMATIONS

Ladies, use the next twenty-one days to decree and declare the ten affirmations below over your life. An optimistic mindset and speech are best compared to a pessimistic mindset and speech, as both have the power to change the trajectory of your life. Scripture informs us, "Death and life are in the power of the tongue, And those who love it *and* indulge it will eat its fruit *and* bear the consequences of their words" (Proverbs 18:21 AMP). Use your words to encourage and motivate yourself as you learn to become your biggest fan and loudest cheerleader.

Twenty-one days is a timeframe that is often referenced in regards to breaking a habit while forming another. I encourage you to establish a new habit in your life and shower yourself with the Word of God. Over time, your brain will replace harmful content with the influx of positive thoughts, words, and beliefs that are implanted. Embrace your new normal as you "Speak It, until You Believe It."

Affirmation #1: I am loved. John 3:16

Affirmation #2: I am beautiful. Song of Solomon 4:7 (NLT)

Affirmation #3: I am wise. Proverbs 31:26

Affirmation #4: I am created for a specific purpose. Ephesians 2:10

Affirmation #5: I am chosen, and I am royalty. 1 Peter 2:9

Affirmation #6: "I am what I am" because of God's grace. 1 Corinthians 15:10

Affirmation #7: "I am fearfully and wonderfully made." Psalm 139:14

Affirmation #8: I am "highly favored" and blessed. Luke 1:28 (NKJV)

Affirmation #9: I am more than a conqueror. Romans 8:37

Affirmation #*10*: I am worth more than rubies.

Proverbs 31:10

How awesome is God and how He spoke so marvelously concerning us? The Bible asks in Romans 8:31: "What, then, shall we say in response to these things? If God is for us, who can be against us?" God is on our side, and these affirmations are intended to empower us as we declare them over our lives. They (affirmations) are sweet reminders of what should consume our thoughts versus the cares of this world. Most importantly, let's return to our first love; as the Bible states, "We love Him because He first loved us" (1 John 4:19 NKJV). The greatest love we will ever know and experience is the love of our Savior and Redeemer, Jesus Christ.

Jesus must become more important, while I become less important.

-John 3:30 (CEV)

8

My Truth and More

I would be remiss if I did not disclose my testimony, beginning with my childhood, my life before accepting Christ, and my continual journey with Christ. I was born and raised in Miami, Florida, by two wonderful parents. I became active in sports at a young age, which started with me running alongside family members' cars as they would leave my home.

One day my older brother said to our mom, "Hey, you need to put her in track and field." My mother took his advice, and before I knew it, I began running track (thank you brother for your insight). Due to my athleticism, I was blessed to receive a track and field scholarship to attend college in North Carolina.

FAR TOO SOON

Although I had a wonderful childhood and enjoyed the simple pleasures of life, my innocence and precious jewel were lost on account of my actions. As an adolescent, sex was common in my peer group. In fact, most girls in school would often express how they felt like a woman from their experience. I attended church occasionally, so I knew God was not pleased with my behavior, and I knew my parents would have been upset with me for losing my virginity. My friends were now women, or so they thought, and I wanted to emulate my peers.

In doing so, it was not until I became much older, as discussed in chapter one, that I began to grasp and comprehend the severity of my actions. The full extent of the emotional/mental harm and remnants associated with premarital sex were unbeknownst to me. Although this activity (sex) is pleasurable, I believe it causes damaging and lasting effects in our lives when it occurs outside of marriage. As a result, wisdom should be utilized when choosing whom to date. Selecting the right person to date does not imply you have received a permit to indulge in sexual relations. The importance lies within having a mutual desire to maintain sexual purity by those in a dating relationship.

Dating and engaging in sex is a universal language that implies; if you are in a relationship as boyfriend and girlfriend, then you must engage in premarital sex. Many couples in dating relationships believe that without sex, there is no real relationship. Not only is this language the primary method of communication, but sex is also the oxygen that breathes life into these relationships.

When the oxygen supply is cut off entirely or reduced to a few times a month, the dating relationship eventually dies. Illustrating how lustful quicksand homes are built instead of applying godly wisdom to avoid "sexual immorality" (1 Corinthians 6:18). This Scripture is not only beneficial for our soul, but it also prevents us from starting a dating relationship in sin.

Nevertheless, this same language and oxygen supply accompanied me throughout my undergraduate years in college. However, one of my teammates exposed me to the truth about Jesus, and after several thought-provoking conversations, I surrendered my life to Christ. Once I surrendered, I joined a great church to further my understanding and knowledge of God. I dedicated my life to Christ when I was a child; therefore, this journey was considered a rededication. The struggle I endured before finally surrendering was very challenging and will be revealed later in this chapter.

THE LIFE I KNEW AND THE ONE I SHOWED

Even though I professed Jesus Christ as my Lord and Savior, I still lived a double life. I had a desire to live for Christ, but I was also not ready to renounce a life of sin. I wanted to find a loophole in my new faith that would enable me to have my cake and eat it too, which would only benefit my flesh and not my spirit.

Before surrendering to Christ, I remember providing a crazy excuse to my teammate as to why the hesitation existed. One night I stated, "I need something bad to happen to me." I even went as far as to say, "I need to be in a car accident or something." My teammate was appalled by my response and replied, "Why do you need that to happen to you?" My response was simple, "Because I do."

Although I provided my teammate with a ridiculous response concerning surrendering, God knew the reason. I literally could not envision living for Him the way He commands us to, especially the command to remain sexually pure as a single person. Total submission to Christ was foreign to me, and the assumed negative responses from others only heightened my level of anxiety regarding a new lifestyle. Being a saved college kid or "Jesus freak" (as some may say) was not cool, in my opinion. After all, I was a few states away from home with no parents in sight; I was living my best life, a life involving freedom and a will to do whatever I desired.

At this point, surrendering appeared more difficult, but as my teammate continued to fellowship and share the gospel with me, I became convicted in my spirit to live a life of holiness. It is often said that your family members or friends may be the only Bible you will read pertaining to the life they live according to God's will. This statement was true regarding my relationship with my teammate.

I struggled to find a balance between living for Christ and continuing to live in sin. My private battle was not apparent from my outer appearance and prompted me to wear two different masks: one around those closest to me and a different one around strangers. The masks were a result of the guilt and shame I carried for having one foot in the church and one foot in the world, also known as being lukewarm. As a newbie in Christ, I desired both worlds. Wherefore, faking my Christian walk was the only thing I knew how to do until I understood what it meant to be a faithful follower of Jesus Christ.

The masks provided the protection and covering I needed from being exposed by my sins. The thought of exposure to those who knew me was extremely frightening. Being labeled a backslider (although I was) or the girl who could not get her life together were matters I did not want to be associated with. No one knew the intricate details of my personal life, which allowed me to live in secrecy.

Many of us have stated, "My business is my business." Yet, the Word of God teaches a very different principle in James 5:16 and states, "Therefore confess your sins to each other and pray for each other so that you may be healed. The prayer of a righteous person is powerful and effective." One is not required to confess their sins to everyone, but you *must* confess your sins (business) to someone to receive the help, healing, and accountability you need for your soul. Living a lie or refusing to come out of darkness is only detrimental to oneself.

Even though I knew these things to be true, wearing my good-girl mask while living in secrecy allowed me to keep everyone at bay. I was able to convince others that I was delivered from fornication and felt as though I had too much to lose. My reputation was more important than revealing my inner struggles, but in the end, I was only digging a deeper pit for myself. While my masks may have fooled people, God was not; as the Bible states, "The eyes of the LORD are everywhere, keeping watch on the wicked and the good" (Proverbs 15:3).

Our testimonies in life are not meant for others to use against us or to shame us, although some may try. They are meant to uplift those who can relate to our story. It behooves us to reveal our deepest, darkest struggles to someone. I did not want anyone to condemn me for not becoming a changed woman immediately after accepting Christ. I needed to fellowship with a loving and patient person who could help me understand my new commitment to the Lord.

To be clear, we all need someone to hold us accountable for our actions and for the edification of our souls; my teammate did precisely that.

If the King of kings and the Lord of lords, Jesus Christ, had twelve men whom He trusted and fellowshipped with daily, surely we too need someone in our lives. Find an individual you can confide in who will help to strengthen and encourage you during your shortcomings (Galatians 6:1). Do not surround yourself with "yes men" or "yes women," as these individuals will only prove harmful to your progression in life. If you are a "yes person" to someone, I strongly encourage you to stop being an enabler. Being a Bible instead is the greatest and most empowering gift you can bestow upon a person, as we are known as "the light of [Christ to] the world" (Matthew 5:14 AMP).

THE COMMITMENT

During this time of rededicating my life to Christ, I was also in a committed relationship, which only complicated matters for me. Suddenly, I was faced with my cake situation as described earlier. I desired to find a loophole in my new faith that would allow me to live for Jesus and maintain a sexual relationship with my boyfriend as well. Of course, this was wishful thinking, but in reality, I was at a crossroad as the tug-of-war continued to weigh heavily upon me. The war within caused tremendous guilt and conviction in my spirit, as it became difficult to live for Jesus while remaining in sin.

Yes! I loved God, but I also lusted after my man, and I did not want to leave him behind. I lusted after him to the point I was willing to delay my submission to Christ. Notice I am saying "lust" and not "love." Being impaired sexually can feel like love, but oftentimes it is lust. I was straddling the fence, trying to find the perfect cake mix to solve my problem.

Simply stated, there is only one way to live when following Christ, and it is His way. One of my pastors once stated, "Whatever you compromise to keep, you will eventually lose in the end." Those words became my reality and my relationship with my boyfriend ended shortly after.

I was free from being sexually impaired after my breakup, and seeking God became much easier. As a result, I created a slogan to help me navigate through my single journey: "I would rather be backed up than burnt up for all eternity." Some of you may understand what I am referring to, and some may be confused. In plain language, I would rather go without premarital sex than suffer the consequences of my sins.

Over the years, my slogan has kept me on firm ground on many occasions. Surrendering to Christ does not mean the temptation to be sexually active or any temptation for that matter will cease. Satan will always be upset over your decision to surrender to Christ. He (Satan) never forgets what sins have kept us in bondage for many years.

It appears as though he (Satan) holds a record of everything we enjoyed that did not involve Christ. Once saved, Satan presents the same temptations to us, but this time they are wrapped in different packages, disguised as gifts. If you are not careful and observant with your spiritual eyes, you will become fooled as the Bible states, "Even Satan disguises himself as an angel of light" (2 Corinthians 11:14 NLT).

For this reason, take your time to inspect your package(s) to determine its origin. Both God and Satan can send people or packages our way, but it is up to us to determine the sender. Anything deterring you away from the will of God is a good indicator that Satan is the originating source. Amid your inspection period, your sender may be revealed immediately, while others may take additional time to discover. Once Satan is revealed as the sender, please return promptly!

After graduating from college, I moved back to Miami briefly and then returned to North Carolina for employment purposes. For the first time, I was alone with no roommates and was excited to embark on my new journey. I was an adult (for real this time) and no longer believed being saved was not cool. I did not know what to expect as a single Christian, but I was committed to following Christ, no matter how challenging the road would become.

Once I moved into my apartment, I remember conversing with a family member who attempted to give me advice on living as a single woman. This individual stated, "You should keep some condoms in your apartment just in case you have a male friend over at some point." I remember my response very vividly as if it were yesterday, and replied: "If I'm trying to live for Christ, then I don't need to tempt myself by having a guy at my home in the first place." While I understood the reasoning and logic behind their comment, I also understood the gravity of my actions.

I did not want to "give the devil a foothold," which God encourages us not to give to him (Satan) in Ephesians 4:27. Having a "movie night" or a "chill moment" with a good-looking guy would only breed an atmosphere of temptation providing a foothold (leverage) to the devil. I needed to be held accountable for my actions. I did not want to fool myself into thinking we were only going to watch a movie and talk . . . yeah right. In other words, refuse to assist Satan in enticing you to sin.

Creating healthy and safe boundaries during dating is a must, proving the importance of accountability. To be clear, not all accountability is good accountability. I am referring to the family member or friend who will hold you accountable for your actions and say, "I know you are trying to live right, and inviting a guy or girl over for some alone time is not in your best interest." Although one may have a good accountability partner, most people do not like the escape plan God has created for them when faced with temptation. The Bible informs us that "No temptation has overtaken you except what is common to mankind. And God is faithful; he will not let you be tempted beyond what you can bear. But when you are tempted, he will also provide a way out so that you can endure it" (1 Corinthians 10:13).

Learning to accept God's escape plan for my life has helped me develop spiritually over the years. As a new Christian, learning not to overthink my progression in Christ, and realizing I was not exempt from temptation, became integral components of my life as well. Scripture states, "Therefore let the one who thinks he stands firm [immune to temptation, being overconfident and self-righteous], take care that he does not fall [into sin and condemnation]" (1 Corinthians 10:12 AMP). Failure to heed my actions gave rise to me begging and pleading with God to remove me from situations I willingly entered into. Taking heed of one's actions varies from person to person. Transforming our minds to the will of God is challenging, (but achievable) mainly because our minds were programmed to the wavelength of sin for so long.

Adopting the mindset of Christ empowers us and prevents our flesh from becoming the dominating force in our lives. To achieve such empowerment and reprogramming of our minds, the Bible states, "Don't copy the behavior and customs of this world, but let God transform you into a new person by changing the way you think. Then you will learn to know God's will for you, which is good and pleasing and perfect" (Romans 12:2 NLT). Additionally, the following lifesavers below will aid in our transformation process by continuing to read His spiritual weapon (the Bible), understanding the power of the mind, creating exit strategies, and praying without ceasing. These four lifesavers should be used in conjunction with one another on a continual basis. When applied, a transformation will be evident in the life of a believer and follower of Jesus Christ.

THE BIBLE

"So faith comes from hearing, that is, hearing the Good News about Christ" (Romans 10:17 NLT). This Scripture informs us the Word of God is the faith-building component we need and must have in our lives. Hence, allowing yourself to hear God's Word daily will help develop your faith in all areas of your life. The Bible even compares our faith to the size of a mustard seed (Matthew 17:20), which is all we need to achieve the things we desire.

The Word of God is powerful, and "All Scripture is inspired by God and is useful to teach us what is true and to make us realize what is wrong in our lives. It corrects us when we are wrong and teaches us to do what is right" (2 Timothy 3:16 NLT). Additionally, "Such things were written in the Scriptures long ago to teach us. And the Scriptures give us hope and encouragement as we wait patiently for God's promises to be fulfilled" (Romans 15:4 NLT). Thus, allow the Word of God to penetrate your heart as you continue to develop and strengthen your faith in Him.

THE MIND

The power of the mind is critical to our commitment to Christ, as we are instructed to "Think about the things of heaven, not the things of earth" (Colossians 3:2 NLT). The Bible also informs us that, "Thou wilt keep *him* in perfect peace, *whose* mind *is* stayed *on thee*: because he trusteth in thee" (Isaiah 26:3 KJV). Romans 12:2 states, "Don't copy the behavior and customs of this world, but let God transform you into a new person by changing the way you think. Then you will learn to know God's will for you, which is good and pleasing and perfect" (NLT). "Finally, brothers and sisters, whatever is true, whatever is noble, whatever is right, whatever is pure, whatever is lovely, whatever is admirable—if anything is excellent or praiseworthy—think about such things" (Philippians 4:8).

The aforementioned Scriptures, and many others, reference the power of the mind. Some people have referred to our minds as the devil's playground and the place he enjoys spending most of his time if not all. However, I am so grateful we serve a mighty and all-knowing God who forewarned us of the importance of where our focus should be. A significant part of our battles in life occurs in our minds, and if we are not careful, we can give life to harmful thoughts. Instead, meditate on the Word of God, which provides encouragement, hope, and strength to conquer everyday challenges.

EXIT STRATEGIES

From a practical standpoint, avoid placing yourself in uncertain or harmful situations as you cultivate and strengthen your faith. Your plan of action may require you to change the company you keep and the places you frequent. You've heard the sayings "birds of a feather flock together" and "show me who your friends are, and I will tell you who you are." Whichever course of action you decide to take, keep in mind the people, places, and things that will trigger (activate) your bondage. Jesus said it best in Luke 9:23 when He stated, "If anyone wishes to follow Me [as My disciple], he must deny himself [set aside selfish interests], and take up his cross daily [expressing a willingness to endure whatever may come] and follow Me [believing in Me, conforming to My example in living and, if need be, suffering or perhaps dying because of faith in Me]" (AMP). Jesus' command to follow Him is the best course of action to emulate in our lives.

PRAYER

The last lifesaver is prayer. The Bible instructs us to "Pray without ceasing" (1Thessalonians 5:17 KJV), which means a continual act. The Bible also states, "Devote yourselves to prayer with an alert mind and a thankful heart." (Colossians 4:2 NLT). Prayer is our open line of communication with God the Father, and we should speak with Him daily. Your battles, big or small, are won through your prayer life. Wherefore, do not underestimate the power and authority God has given you.

As you are aware, addressed within this book are the topics of dating and sex. I would like to provide an example of what not to do concerning prayer and sex. If you decide to remain abstinent until the wedding night, then do not begin to pray for strength to resist fornicating when a guy or girl is en route to your home. You and I can agree that this particular prayer may not be effective. When trying to overcome sin, you must pray daily for the strength to win the battle. Additionally, take responsibility for your actions and avoid tempting situations.

Your prayers to God for strength to overcome sexual immorality, or any area of sin, should be transparent and authentic. The Bible states, "Even before there is a word on my tongue [still unspoken], Behold, O LORD, You know it all" (Psalm 139:4 AMP). God knows everything anyway, so why not receive help from the One who loves you unconditionally? Never be afraid to go before God in prayer and admit your temptations. Disclose all weaknesses and ask Him to give you His strength and willpower, **NOT** to engage in sin. God desires to help us, and "If we confess our sins, He is faithful and just to forgive us *our* sins and to cleanse us from all unrighteousness" (1 John 1:9 NKJV).

Additionally, the finished work of Jesus Christ on the cross at Calvary has redeemed us and made us more than a conqueror (Romans 8:37 AMP). Being more than a conqueror is evidence we can overcome sin. The shed blood of Christ has equipped everyone with the ability and power to win, as His power (the cross) is not limited, nor shall it be selective to our choosing. More importantly, the power of the cross is the undergirding (strength) that empowers us to live the life we are destined to live.

SIMPLY PUT, SIN SEPARATES

Though God is faithful and just to forgive us when we sin, I have learned from studying the Word (Bible) that continuing in sin was damaging my relationship with Him. As a result, I became separated from God and was spiritually dead. I believed I was alive (spiritually) because I functioned as a living person; however, this was not truthful. A spiritual death is similar to what Adam and Eve experienced when they ate the forbidden fruit in Genesis. They did not die physically, but were spiritually dead and separated from God.

God loves us dearly, but our sin separates us from Him and interferes with our relationship with Him. The Bible states, "But your iniquities have separated you from your God; And your sins have hidden *His* face from you, So that He will not hear" (Isaiah 59:2 NKJV). To reiterate, we must confess our sins to God to be forgiven by Him. Once we confess our sins, the Bible states, "there is joy in the presence of the angels of God over one sinner who repents [that is, changes his inner self—his old way of thinking, regrets past sins, lives his life in a way that proves repentance; and seeks God's purpose for his life]" (Luke 15:10 AMP). Through repentance and the help of the Holy Spirit, we are guided back into right standing before God.

As previously stated, Adam became separated from God due to sin. This separation began when God asked Adam, "Where are you?" (Genesis 3:9), immediately after he sinned. The question posed by the all-knowing God was not inquiring about Adam's geographical location in the garden, especially when God placed him there. Instead, the question posed was concerning Adam's spiritual location, and for the first time in his life, he became separated from God. Knowing Adam sinned, I believe God asked him where he was located (spiritually) to ensure Adam understood the severity of his actions and the disconnect that would subsequently follow.

In fact, Jesus Himself also experienced being separated from God when He carried our sins to the cross. "And about the ninth hour Jesus cried with a loud voice, saying, Eli, Eli, lama sabachthani? that is to say, My God, my God, why hast thou forsaken me?" (Matthew 27:46 KJV). For the first time in Jesus' life, He became separated from God. The separation occurred as He hung on the cross on our behalf and was made a sinner for our sake (2 Corinthians 5:21).

Due to Jesus' sacrifice on the cross, "In him we have redemption through his blood, the forgiveness of sins, in accordance with the riches of God's grace" (Ephesians 1:7). Though our sins were paid in full by Jesus Christ, and we were spared from the wrath of God, we do not have permission to indulge in sin. The vast majority of us have used God's grace and forgiving nature to our sinful advantage. Proof of such advantage is found in Romans 6:15, when the Bible checks our motives and asks, "Well then, since God's grace has set us free from the law, does that mean we can go on sinning? Of course not!" (NLT).

Jesus paid the ultimate price for our sins with His life in order for us to have a life (John 10:10). Do not hope for something traumatic to happen to you as I foolishly desired before surrendering to Christ.

During that season of my life, I did not want to forsake the pleasures of this world and believed all possible fun was lost. However, the Bible states, "look not at the things which are seen, but at the things which are unseen; for the things which are visible are temporal [just brief and fleeting], but the things which are invisible are everlasting *and* imperishable" (2 Corinthians 4:18 AMP).

FORGIVENESS AND SALVATION ARE THE GOALS

Now let's fast-forward to a different season of my life. As mentioned in chapter one, I am divorced. I met my ex-husband while in college, and we often kept in touch over the years. Eventually, we began a long-distance relationship, as I was living and working in North Carolina at the time. After dating for several months, he proposed prompting me to relocate back to Florida. We were married shortly after and embraced becoming one. A few years later, we welcomed our little queen. However, our union did not last; thus, remaining optimistic about my future was (is) essential.

If you are divorced, use this season of your life to heal, love, discover and appreciate yourself for the man or woman you were created to be. Place all trust and confidence in God as He cares immensely for your soul. Do not give up on yourself simply because an earthly relationship has run its course; rather live confidently, knowing greatness is within you. More importantly, you were created in the image of God (Genesis 1:27).

As your healing journey begins, refrain from harboring hatred and unforgiveness in your heart towards your ex. Believe it or not, you are only hurting yourself, as God will not forgive you of your sins if you have not forgiven others of their sins (Matthew 6:15).

Forgiveness is mainly for self and not for the other person. "Above all, love each other deeply, because love covers over a multitude of sins" (1 Peter 4:8).

Sometimes we display signs of selective memory and cannot recall the mess God removed us from. His amazing love did not expose our shortcomings to others (love covers sins). Not only am I grateful for His love, but I am also thankful that "he does not treat us as our sins deserve or repay us according to our iniquities" (Psalm 103:10). God is kind and gracious towards us even when we are undeserving of such mercy.

Never allow anger, rage, or bitterness to interfere with your commandment to love. I get it; some people are difficult to love because they are vindictive, spiteful, manipulative, selfish, evil, and the list goes on, but this is why prayer is so vital in the life of a believer. Our strength has limitations, but the Holy

Spirit does not, and what we are incapable of doing, He will do for us. With His help, we are able to love those we deem unlovable.

Despite your marriage ending, your life has not, and God still has great work for you to accomplish. Jesus informed us in John 14:12 that we would perform the works He has done and even greater because He had to return to the Father. God holds the blueprint for your life, and only He can reveal His plans for you. Return to the Creator to receive guidance and direction in respect to the next chapter in your life.

You may experience a range of emotions concerning the next chapter of your life, and areas of uncertainty are frightening and cause doubt. Nevertheless, "know [with great confidence] that God [who is deeply concerned about us] causes all things to work together [as a plan] for good for those who love God, to those who are called according to His plan *and* purpose" (Romans 8:28 AMP). Amid our trials and tribulations, God can use all things (good or bad) to work together for our good. Additionally, when you are terrified, frightened, or discouraged, know that "the LORD your God will be with you wherever you go" (Joshua 1:9).

Though uncertain in the beginning concerning my relationship with Jesus, surrendering my life to Him was the best decision I have ever made. Over time, I learned that perfection was not a prerequisite to becoming a follower of Christ. The saying "come as you are" is not solely based on your outer garments, as some may believe, but rather on the current state of your life and the affairs of your heart. "But God showed his great love for us by sending Christ to die for us while we were still sinners" (Romans 5:8 NLT).

The Romans Scripture dispels the idea of perfection as God showered us with love by sending

Jesus to die for us. Think, if we were perfect would we need a Savior? Do not become fixated on making things "right" in your life before surrendering to Christ. In fact, you can accept the gift of salvation today by declaring "with your mouth, 'Jesus is Lord,' and believe in your heart that God raised him from the dead, you will be saved" (Romans 10:9). Remember, your walk with Christ is a daily journey, but each journey begins with a yes and a willing heart.

And yet, O LORD, you are our Father. We are the clay, and you are the potter. We all are formed by your hand.

-Isaiah 64:8 (NLT)

Prayer

Heavenly Father, I thank You for this day. I come before You on behalf of Your many sons and daughters that You have created, and I pray they will begin to envision themselves as You do. I pray they will never allow anyone to tear them down with words contrary to Your truth about them. Father, I pray Your sons and daughters will not only walk in greatness, but in the authority You have given them. I pray they will no longer live a life that is pleasing to their flesh, but will raise their standards in life and take a stand for what they know is pleasing and acceptable in Your sight. Father, I pray You will continue to disrupt the forces of darkness as Your light continues to prevail. Father, I thank you that You do not seek perfection, but You seek progression as we turn our hearts towards You. I pray we do not interpret your patience as a sign of acceptance to sin, but that we view your patience as longsuffering as we yearn for eternal life with You. I pray we will become better ambassadors for You as we show the world that You are and will always be the answer for it. I pray we experience an everlasting love that loves us unconditionally. Father God, I am speaking of a love that You give at all times. And now, "The LORD bless thee, and keep thee: The LORD make his face shine upon thee, and be gracious unto thee: The LORD lift up his countenance upon thee, and give thee peace" (Numbers 6:24–26 KJV). Be blessed, God's children, in the days, months, and years to come. In Jesus' matchless name, I pray. Amen.

www.ingramcontent.com/pod-product-compliance
Lightning Source LLC
Chambersburg PA
CBHW030304100526
44590CB00012B/521